# Backyard Wonder

# Other Books by Paddy Fievet

*When Life Cried Out: One Woman's Spiritual Quest to Be Fully Alive*

*The Making of a Mystic: Writing as a Form of Spiritual Emergence*

*The Eagle's View: Five Steps to Modern Mysticism*

Available at Amazon.com

# Backyard Wonder

PADDY FIEVET

BackYardPoetrySeries@gmail.com

Copyright © 2025 Paddy Fievet
Printed in the United States of America
First Edition Trade Book, 2025

ISBN 979-8-218-71375-1

Library of Congress Control Number: 2025914030

Published in Hilton Head Island, South Carolina

Editorial: Kerry Wade, kerriganwade.com
Proofreading, Design, Publishing assistance: Tell Tell Poetry

First Printing, 2025

Dedicated to seekers gloriously noticing
the Divinity of all creation.

# Contents

# Acknowledgments

Heartfelt thanks to Kerry Wade (www.kerriganwade.com), an extraordinary poetry editor who managed to take my initial poetry and put it into readable form. Without the help of Kallie Falandays of Tell Tell Poetry (www.telltellpoetry.com), I seriously doubt this project would have gotten beyond a computer file and a drawer full of handwritten poetic musings. Working with her and her staff has been a treasure. A heartfelt thanks to Dr. Susan Russell of the Atlanta area, whose wisdom and expertise became invaluable in my journey to true self. Most of all, it is with heartfelt appreciation that I thank my loving husband Chris who has patiently listened to parts of my poetry, often one or two lines at a time and often before his first cup of coffee, as I write best in the wee hours of beginning daylight. Sweetheart, you are the best.

# Preface

Words in red pen
upon lined notebook—
first draft,
of course—
without proper spacing
angles
metric dance
or interlocutory meaning.

Unsurpassed connection.

Not my words,
naturally,
yet snippets of an eternal divinity
arranged in nature's chaotic community

through my poet's heart.

Keep your proper rules and regulations—
greatness always oozes from the heart,
not the mind.
Spirit dances through every expressive letter,
trills within each word—

a flaming combustion of Love.

# Introduction

When the awakening rays of sunlight explode over the rivers, peek through the pines, and bathe my soul with nature's glory at the beginning of each day, the writer within me always wants to put words to the splendor I feel.

When the blackberry lilies open their throated petals, when the dolphin rolls in the sea, and when the flutter of a passing butterfly touches my heart, I endeavor to place their innate Wonder on the pages of my notebooks. My best results rarely come from linear thoughts, but from a Oneness of all creation, realized only through the heart. Over the years, I have learned only poetry allows the multidimensional Spirit of nature to fit gloriously upon the two-dimensional page. Poetry expresses well the grandeur of nature formed from ordinary words.

I've never sought a poem, never sat down in front of a computer screen to purposely write a collection; honestly, I don't think I could. Instead, this writing came to me through feelings, or rather from outside of me, through me, to be shared with you. As you read these poems, read them not as formal poetry with conventional rules, cadence, and order, but understand them as nature's unique essence grafted into love. Open your heart long enough to feel each poem's glory.

Looking back upon my life's journey, I smile, realizing at age twenty, thirty, and even forty, I didn't have the ability to deeply feel what nature bestowed. Perhaps gentle recognition comes with age, with wisdom of living while adoring the innate essence of the world around me. At least, it happened that way for me. Consider these poems nature's way of sharing tidbits of grandeur, tidbits of that glorious wonder available to all. Read, absorb, incorporate as you wish.

Profound glory awaits in the most seemingly infinitesimal soul of nature's majesty.

# Backyard Wonder

# Beckoning

The poetry of early morning—
*no words necessary*—
rising orange and yellow blaze
reaching through pine limbs
stretching outward into pleasantness.
Butterflies fluttering into their delight.
Flower petals titillate with loving glory.

One old iron table,
fresh paint cradling memories,
four chairs,
a book of delicious poetry
and my favorite cup of tea

all perfectly set to awaken
the glorious Spirit—
ours for the beckoning.

# Upon Awaking

Water rushes through the creek bed
at bubbling breakneck speed
just as sunlight begins to differentiate light and shadow.

Yesterday's abundance overflows the banks
while welcoming murmurs explode into a screaming stream.

What's the hurry, I wonder.

*Has the coffee perked yet?*

# Ambition

Why are the birds singing?
The hills rise into early morning

as sunlight wisps of promise
streak between clouds while
painting patches of yellow on treetops
rising from fields of splendor green

with open attitudes.
Life's song raptures from yellow-throated warblers,
too enthralled with the morning
to think of the chores awaiting the day.

While I, with cup in hand,
beg the steaming coffee to give me reason
to get out of the comfortable, overstuffed chair
covered with a faded wildflower meadow.

I pause,
listening…

The warbling chorus with their song of ambition
enthralls the simplicity of each breath.
Beauty lies in the promise of each exhalation
and intake fills the soul
with sunlight, rolling hills, green grasses—

All that goodness, all that glory
for the coming day.

# This Lovely Day

The to-do list sits plump and proud
commandingly on the kitchen counter,
obscenely ordinary.

The real poetry lies through the glass doors
where daffodils shoot toward spring
and acorns embrace oak tree potential.

Today I must let my heartbeat
meander along exuberantly,
engulf myself in the present.

*Now* is my poetry:
multi-dimensional breaths of acute joy
swirling across a two-dimensional to-do list,
laughing heartily at the meaningless absurdities.

# Making Love with the Rain

Cell phone news
does not suit today.

I shove it vigorously
across the table
where it clangs to the floor—
a noisy cacophony of sordid tales,
myriad ways everyone
doesn't love anyone.

Gentle rain seeps through the air
like tears.

*Yet,*
*yet still,*
*could this thought be true?*

Perhaps the rain is nature's cleansing,
washing our intentions fresh.
A baptism,
despite ourselves.

I don't wish to think of worldly things this morning.
Only how the raindrops feel
as they congregate in my hair,
slide off my skin
like rushing mountain streams,
collecting in puddles
around my ankles
before oozing through the wooden
cracks of the kitchen deck.

# Choice

*Some* mornings scream their intentions
suffocated with distressful human meanderings.
Will the banks fail again?
Is the new variant a concern?
How polluted is my water?
Are the children safe?

*Other* mornings are meant for being,
reaching out luscious fingers,
tickling hearts of those awakened enough to feel,
blowing aside thunderous problems—
they are only dead leaves
falling from moss enriched wild oaks.

*Special* mornings are absorbable glory,
beckoning me along opportunities
to breathe deeply,
to feel Presence gloriously,
to fondle all the real beauty.

These mornings are so alive,
filled with Total Presence.

*Some mornings.*
*Other mornings.*
*Special mornings.*

Giggle with the choice.

# Evolving

Dunes of sand build,
forever recede,
reformulate themselves continually.

In an uproar, the sea commands
and the sandbanks accommodate
redistribution of shape and form,
present in a different way,
in a different place,
recognizable only as an inner longing
of life shifting in wider aplomb.

I hurry through my days,
wondering if time finally will slow
with changes of insight bursting forth
from my own divinity.
I seek greater wisdom.

Relationships ebb and flow.
Choices create themselves anew.
I behold a wider landscape
within the consciousness of my inner knowing.

Seeds of fortitude grace
my changing blessing,
not as I was,
not as I will be
but fully present within the ocean's breeze.

# The Essential Garden

As the dawn of a morning
twinkles sweet kisses
through the fluttery pear blossoms
just outside the bedroom window,
surges of light and shadow permeate
the heart of my soul. I awaken.

The light from without
meets a forthright glow within
entwining surety of connection
as the Bougainvillea wraps itself
on the garden trellis of my thoughts.

A new perspective blossoms in fragrant delight—
dancing in the sunshine,
meditating through the shadows.
tendrils of Spirit growing in the Eden of my soul.

# My World

Oh, to live
in a glass house
on a hill surrounded
by forests where the gentle world
comes to the door

through roaming streams.
Where raccoons wash
and the owl hunts
while the deer tiptoe
through flower beds, pausing only
for roses, petunias, and daylilies.

This is the world I inhabit well
without news intending to shock
or politicians demanding money
I don't have to give.
What joy in pausing to watch the flowers bloom.

# Delight

Early morning promises
filter through the branches,
as light dances upon the leaves
before pirouetting to me
for me
with me.
Green leaves against the blue sky
mingle with love
joy
and potential so profound
even the gentle breeze laughs merrily.

# Today

Isn't this lovely!
There's so much to do
yet the leaves are exquisitely beautiful
with gold, bronze, and crimson
dancing wonderfully.

# Intensity

Something great or insignificant must like the heat,
must be thrilled God created fiery air so intense
birds sing only at night, gators submerge themselves
beneath lagoon waters which
never cool.

Frilly daisy petals wilt before finally giving up
falling like molten lava rocks
to the soil to decay
feeding the seeds that thrive in the oppressive warmth.

Early this morning at the dock
I welcomed the sun
into this world again.
Shine brightly! Send
your intense, golden rays down
once again
that this special heat-loving thing—
whatever it is —
grows into living light
within the burn.

# Magnificent Life

O, you beautiful life
I'm here—
right here—twirling,
twirling, evolving slowly
with hands upraised to soul fluttering
rays of sunshine.

O, you exquisite life
cresting within,
within me—imploding.
Take charge,
abound
with love cascading

so when I touch
the buttercup,
insignificance turns into all.

# Spirit's Chorus

A yellow-throated warbler chose the barest of rhododendrons
as a perch to sing of love. Not ten feet from my rocking chair,
his song expressed depth and clarity of Spirit adoration
while my own world was sodden with gloom.
Graced by his presence, for a moment his cheer
unobtrusively dispelled my own disquietude
as I glided among the pluming notes
to find a more peaceful self-refrain.

# Heartfelt Hearing

God is singing today.
I know this to be true,
though my ears are old
and for the most part useless.

I still hear Divine notes
ringing a sweet chorus
through the silence.

Trees provide accompaniment
and the daffodils raise their horns
standing proud through the earth.
Otter raises his head
throning this way and that.
I saw his smile in God's refrain.

While I,
hearing best with my wide-open heart,
am thankful for less human chatter
as nature bathes my soul.

# The Iris Blossom

Come, little one,
open your colors
past sleeping insignificance,
making real
promises of splendor
as petals spread
like open psalms
celebrating pure glory.

# Trust

Soft paws peer around
the brick corner of the den
before scampering off when I call.

Narrow, watchful eyes discern safety,
wonder about trust.

When I rattle the pan of kitty food,
suddenly, we are best friends.

Trust is simply a matter of hunger.

# Late Bloomer

Fiery red roses cluster
their blooms on short, leafy stems,
twittering fingers reaching
toward the watery pond. Ten bushes
awaken each spring, chorusing
through summer, preparing to sleep.

On the end of the row, singular to itself,
a silent friend watches, hovers
to herself: a compacted dome,
a late bloomer. Only when midsummer
blaze touches the earth
does she open. Green
to white, transforming
to pink frills

not in abundance, in delicate wisps,
singular, remnants of rose quartz flashing
gently to only the most mystical observer.
A sensitive soul dares to hold her own
in an explosive red world.

# Curious Rabbit

*Just who are you*, he asks,
nose twitching, dark eyes
glowing out soft brown fur.
He pauses so still,
eyes imploring
long ears shoot upright
two antennae attuned.

Quietly, he witnesses my own stillness
in the early morning glow
before scampering off
to nibble more
out of life.

# Spirit Giggles

Joy steals solidarity from life's mundane events
with pleasure, contentment, and fertile repose
blooming with gay abandonment

*leaves falling on a sunny fall day*
*fuzzy kitties enjoying a tummy rubdown*
*a November jeweled with assured azalea blossoms*
*pizza at breakfast and eggs for dinner*
*hair tasseled by windy whispers*
*long walks under starry twinkles*
*nature's abandon littering a driveway after a storm*
*a dancing glance between two lovers*
*last night's memories and today's trust*
*tenderly holding the hand of my Love*

Sequins of light on a life well lived.

# The Journey

Beside a rushing creek,
mesmerized by the sounds of water bubbling
over,
around,
through clusters of moss-covered rock,
I wonder:

*At its point of origin, does the water know the destination?*

*Or is it simply about the journey?*

Do I know myself?

# The Ocean Within

Hidden depths
with unimaginable secrets
exposed on the shore
as rippling waves reach forth
like long open hands
teasing passersby into believing
their moving expression represents an entirety.

A smile among the crowd
becomes only a surface expression
while the fathoms bespeak
a love true story:
hidden recesses

the divine expression
of the ocean within.

# Divine Timing

The mountain laurel covering the mountainside
just above the chorusing creek
seems so still—
almost compliant:
life as patience.

Yet, in due time it will appear
as a blooming hallelujah!

Then even the stream will applaud.

# Transformation

*An intuitive thing, really*
to wrap in silken threads
while bonded to the tiny twig in a flowing branch
of nature's tendrils

to slowly experience caterpillar legs disappear—
a body turning liquid,
the chrysalis transformation,
a total meltdown
from what was,
unknown from what will be
except only in spiritual desire

to free from confining thoughts
useful no longer
as the watery purpose of life
flows into substance
seeking freedom into being

to witness wings of personal empowerment
stretch outward,
flutter upward,
propel downward,
glistening as sun sparks fresh life
through a soul's expansive gleanings

to fly freely
on wings of Spirit,
from beauty to beauty
and back again
through self-transformation
and the wonders of Creator's love.

# Breath

Wind carries the breath of God
through rustling leaves,
and the rippling of ocean waves.

I reach out, but it playfully blows
between my fingers, effervescent

it carries strands of my hair
across my face in expressions
of opinionated delight

then blows past,
furling into itself as the stillness of God
within. Presence.

# Wisdom of Shaggy Birch

I wander among the trees—
poplar, oak, maple tall
with roots and branches reaching
wide to accept as much life as possible.

In their midst shaggy birch
stand, peeling bark loosening
as if they, like me, have outgrown their own skin.

Do they not feel the anxiety, the fear
of life's interlinking changes as age fosters
special wisdom not fitting
into the smooth, naive bodies of youth?

Insight requires wrinkles, knowing eyes,
gray hair and an acceptance of body fluff.
The greatest shaggy birch laughs to itself
while I pause, listening as it says

*Growth initiates process.*
*Let the old split, peel, and fall away.*
*Emerge.*

I inhale. I breathe. I laugh
as I stroll this old body of mine
down the forest path.

# The Sacred World

I live in two worlds
often simultaneously,
sometimes in conflict.

The world of people grasping,
coercing, shoving attitudes
at each other

warriors hurdling rocks,
which makes me
want to scream.

*Do they not hear
the sacred whispering
poetry and love?*

The world inclusive
where trees intertwine roots
and branches quietly communicate,
rocks swell with gladness,
and the soil is filled
with such potential.

Mother Earth,
let me thrive in your arms.
Wrap around this old body
crafted of flesh and water
until I leave it with you
to soar the cosmos,
blessedly consecrated
in non-world potential and love.

# Yearning

The sea oats whirl
to an unsung tune,
blowing in syncopated beats,
the dance of spirit enlivened—

a yearning inherent.

# Reprocessing

An entire woodland lies before me
meandering up the mountainside.
Oaks, pines, poplars, sycamore friends—
individual expressions of forest life.

I notice only the three deaths—
grey branches tangled among themselves
awaiting nature's ax
in preparation of a grand horizontal grounding.

Perhaps their message is more—
with a deep presence lingering in my own attitude—
than selective environmental recycling.

My inner shadow tries to play
within my conscious thoughts,
dragging me down an unresponsive gloom.

Since my own thoughts are totally of my own doing,
I pick myself off the forest floor of my own mind—
a reprocessing of my own consciousness—
knowing that I can do better than this.

I choose to do better.

# Solitude

Solitude can be a noisy cacophony
if we are not present enough
to hear its tranquil song.

# Oak Tree Nurture

Grandmother stood firm—well-rooted security—arms reaching around her, longing fingers and leafy nails twittering in spring breezes. Spanish moss adorns, a laughing profusion of lace.

*Admiration.*

Come to me, Child, she soothes, love gushing forth as jade flutters against an azure sky. Nestle your sorrows against my heart so I may envelop you.

*All will be well.*

# Absolute Presence

The gentle withstanding leaf
whose life spans only three seasons
before it browns,
withers,
crumples into the soil,

nonetheless stands pure,
blocking the almighty
everlasting potency of the sun
from touching earth
within the perimeters of its protection:
the shadow.

# Woodland Prophets

Grandmothers and grandfathers once
stood their forest presence
before time reset life's cycle—
natural bridges across a scuttling stream
and wooded wonders angled unnaturally in life's bed.
Potential is filled with younger counterparts—
tall and limbless,
leafy expressions culminating just short of the sun.

Humanity could learn from these trees:
*How civilization creates our own shadows*
*while simultaneously competing for the light.*

Silent prophets,
cycling through time.

# Everywhere

*somewhere*

a stream cascades beyond its rocky plateau
falling into the pond below with temporary turbulence.

the stifling heat of August bows in submission to a cool breeze
fluttering leaves joyously dancing within the blowing tune.

gentle flakes of white precariously perch themselves
upon the frozen mountain's peak, a holy reunion.

two feathered lovers crest beside a rippling water's edge
as commitment begins a procreative expression.

dolphins gently surface just before arching into deeper fathoms
of the ocean's loving nurturance.

I remain *nowhere* in particular,
my Spirit soars cosmically into infinite acuity
resting in love's gentle repose slightly beyond the present time—

*everywhere.*

# Enriched

Who could not be
bathed in love,
clothed in divinity,
as the white heron
glides effortlessly
across the pond?

A pureness so palpable
reaches out to greet
my outstretched hand—
my open heart—
feathered angel alighting nearby.

My walk can wait.
I stand so still,
dissipating into Presence.

Heron lands,
moves gracefully
toward a watery dinner table.

I walk on.

# Flowing

A leaf falls gently from its poplar home,
gliding safely to the center of the meandering creek
as if it realized assuredly
emotional flow is a safe place to be.

Can I be as trusting in my own moody surrender
to the ordained experience of life?

Will I allow myself to flow lovingly
through my own emotional presence—
not overwhelmed by tears of sadness, fear or anger,
but simply float in the flowing ripples of life
knowing all is in order?

*All is truly in order*
*the Spirit flows—*
Even leaves know it is so.

# Glory

God's breath flows
through the tree branches
filled with grace.
One only must be visually still,
profoundly witnessing.

Even the leaves participate,
clapping vigorously
in verdant alleluias.

# Joy of Being

Perhaps the oak's roots
must reach into the earthen
bowels of hell

before understanding freely
how beautiful is the light.

Limbs worship in soft winds
filled and reaching
with open arms in grace,

knowing fully
the joy of being alive.

# Magnificent Life

O wild, beautiful life,
I'm here—
right here
twirling slowly
with hands upraised to the soul fluttering
rays of sunshine.

O beautiful life
cresting within,
implode within me,
take charge
with love
so, when I touch the simplicity of tiny buttercups,
insignificance turns into
*Everything.*

O beautiful love.

# Breathe

*I breathe in*
all colors of the Universe.

*I breathe out,*
renewed.

# About the Author

Born to be a seeker of deeper meanings, greater spiritual connection, and that wisdom found in the depths of soul-to-soul contact, Paddy Fievet loved her childhood oak tree, pansy garden with the glorious faces in each flower, and a tiny playhouse, all nurturing her highly sensitive demeanor. Through the twists and turns of life, she meandered away from this special Spiritual connection as she married, raised children, and well-survived a traumatic life upheaval. Wanting to reconnect to the innate wisdom of her childhood, she traveled the world seeking parts of herself she had closed off for decades while trying to fit into a very confining box. During the traveling years, she wrote all manner of things, including articles of self-exploration, poetry, essays about the world—familiar and yet to be discovered. In her early fifties, she obtained a PhD in Metaphysics, a process undertaken for the sole purpose of learning how she fit into this world. Now in her mid-seventies, she is happily remarried with fabulous adult children and lovely grandchildren. Paddy and her husband love living in the Low Country of South Carolina, nurtured mystically by the moss flowing through the oaks, the herons, and the murmur of daily tidal changes teeming with life — a poet's garden. Her life has blossomed, full circle.